The Ginkgo Light

The Ginkgo Light

ARTHUR SZE

Copper Canyon Press
Port Townsend, Washington

Printed in the United States of America

Cover art: Pat Steir, *Yellow and Blue One-Stroke Waterfall,* 1992. 173½ × 90¾ inches, oil on canvas. Collection of the Solomon R. Guggenheim Museum.

Copper Canyon Press is in residence at Fort Worden State Park in Port Townsend, Washington, under the auspices of Centrum. Centrum is a gathering place for artists and creative thinkers from around the world, students of all ages and backgrounds, and audiences seeking extraordinary cultural enrichment.

LIBRARY OF CONGRESS CATALOGING-IN-PUBLICATION DATA

Sze, Arthur.
The ginkgo light / Arthur Sze.
    p. cm.
Includes bibliographical references.
ISBN 978-1-55659-299-7 (pbk.: alk. paper)
I. Title.
PS3569.Z38G56 2009
811´.54—dc22

                                                        2009003972

COPPER CANYON PRESS
Post Office Box 271
Port Townsend, Washington 98368

www.coppercanyonpress.org

for Carol
for Micah and Sarah

ACKNOWLEDGMENTS

Grateful acknowledgment is made to the editors of the following publications in which these poems, sometimes in earlier versions, first appeared:

American Letters & Commentary: "Qualia"

Atlas (New Delhi): "After Completion"

Boston Review: "Pig's Heaven Inn"

Carnet de Route (Paris): "Chrysalis"

Conjunctions: "The Double Helix," "After Completion"

Field: "The Ginkgo Light"

The Georgia Review: "The Gift," "In the Rose Light"

Gulf Coast: "Crisscross," "Tesserae"

Hotel Parnassus: Poetry International 2007 (De Arbeiderspers): "The Gift," translated into Dutch by K. Michel

The Kenyon Review: "Spectral Line"

Language for a New Century: Contemporary Poetry from the Middle East, Asia, and Beyond (Norton): "Labrador Tea"

Mānoa: "Labrador Tea," "Departures and Arrivals," "Fractal," "Yardangs"

Narrative Magazine: "Pig's Heaven Inn," "Grand Bay"

The New Yorker: "Looking Back on the Muckleshoot Reservation from Galisteo Street, Santa Fe"

No: A Journal of the Arts: "Equator," "Pinwheel," "Power Line"

Ploughshares: "Chrysalis"

Poetry Daily (online): "Pig's Heaven Inn," "The Ginkgo Light," "Spectral Line"

The Poetry Foundation Web site: "Chrysalis"

Runes: "Virga"

Shenandoah: "Retrieval"

The Virginia Quarterly Review: "The North Window"

"The Gift," "In the Rose Light," "Qualia," and section 3 of "Spectral Line" appeared, thanks to Tom Leech, as hand-marbled letterpress broadsides from The Press at the Palace of the Governors.

I would also like to thank the City of Santa Fe Arts Commission for support through the poet laureate program.

Thank you, Mei-mei Berssenbrugge, Jon Davis, Carol Moldaw, and Michael Wiegers for close readings of these poems.

Contents

The Ginkgo Light

Chrysalis

Corpses push up through thawing permafrost

as I scrape salmon skin off a pan at the sink;
on the porch, motes in slanting yellow light

undulate in air. Is Venus at dusk as luminous
as Venus at dawn? Yesterday I was about to

seal a borax capsule angled up from the bottom

of a decaying exterior jamb when I glimpsed
jagged ice floating in a bay. Naval sonar

slices through whales, even as a portion
of male dorsal fin is served to the captain

of an umiak. Stopped in traffic, he swings from

a chairlift, gazes down at scarlet paintbrush.
Moistening an envelope before sealing it,

I recall the slight noise you made when I
grazed your shoulder. When a frost wiped out

the chalk blue flowering plant by the door,

I watered until it revived from the roots.
The song of a knife sharpener in an alley

passes through the mind of a microbiologist
before he undergoes anesthesia for surgery.

The first night of autumn has singed

bell peppers by the fence, while budding
chamisa stalks in the courtyard bend to ground.

Observing people conversing at a nearby table,
he visualizes the momentary convergence

and divergence of lines passing through a point.

The wisteria along the porch never blooms;
a praying mantis on the wood floor sips water

from a dog bowl. Laughter from upstairs echoes
downstairs as teenage girls compare bra sizes.

An ex–army officer turned critic frets

over the composition of a search committee,
snickers and disparages rival candidates.

A welder, who turns away for a few seconds
to gaze at the Sangre de Cristos, detects a line

of trucks backed up on an international overpass

where exhaust spews onto houses below.
The day may be called One Toothroad or Six Thunderpain,

but the naming of a day will not transform it,
nor will the mathematics of time halt.

An imprint of ginkgo leaf—fan-shaped, slightly

thickened, slightly wavy on broad edge, two-
lobed, with forking parallel veins but no

midvein—in a slab of coal is momentary beauty,
while ginkgoes along a street dropping gold

leaves are mindless beauty of the quotidian.

Once thought extinct, the ginkgo
was discovered in Himalayan monasteries

and propagated back into the world. Although
I cannot save a grasshopper singed by frost

trying to warm itself on a sunlit walkway,

I ponder shadows of budding pink and orange
bougainvilleas on a wall. As masons level sand,

lay bricks in horizontal then vertical pairs,
we construct a ground to render a space

our own. As light from a partial lunar eclipse

diffuses down skylight walls, we rock and
sluice, rock and sluice, fingertips fanned

to fanned fingertips, debouch into plenitude.
Venus vanishes in a brightening sky:

the diamond ring of a solar eclipse persists.

You did not have to fly to Zimbabwe in June 2001
to experience it. The day recalls Thirteen Death

and One Deer when an end slips into a beginning.
I recall mating butterflies with red dots on wings,

the bow of a long liner thudding on waves,

crescendo of water beginning to boil in a kettle,
echoes of humpback whales. In silence, dancers

concentrate on movements onstage; lilacs bud
by a gate. As bits of consciousness constellate,

I rouse to a 3 A.M. December rain on the skylight.

A woman sweeps glass shards in a driveway,
oblivious to elm branches reflected on windshields

of passing cars. Juniper crackles in the fireplace;
flukes break the water as a whale dives.

The path of totality is not marked by

a shadow hurtling across the earth's surface
at three thousand kilometers per hour.

Our eyelashes attune to each other.
At the mouth of an arroyo, a lamb skull

and ribcage bleach in the sand; tufts

of fleece caught on barbed wire vanish.
The Shang carved characters in the skulls

of their enemies, but what transpired here?
You do not need to steep turtle shells

in blood to prognosticate clouds. Someone

dumps a refrigerator upstream in the riverbed
while you admire the yellow blossoms of

a golden rain tree. A woman weeds, sniffs
fragrance from a line of onions in her garden;

you scramble an egg, sip oolong tea.

The continuous bifurcates into the segmented
as the broken extends. Someone steals

a newspaper while we doze. A tiger
swallowtail lands on a patio columbine;

a single agaric breaks soil by a hollyhock.

Pushing aside branches of Russian olives
to approach the Pojoaque River, we spot

a splatter of flicker feathers in the dirt.
Here chance and fate enmesh.

Here I hold a black bowl rinsed with tea,

savor the warmth at my fingertips,
aroma of emptiness. We rock back and forth,

back and forth on water. Fins of spinner
dolphins break the waves; a whale spouts

to the north-northwest. What is not impelled?

Yellow hibiscus, zodiac, hairbrush;
barbed wire, smog, snowflake—when I still

my eyes, the moments dilate. Rain darkens
gravel in the courtyard; shriveled apples

on branches are weightless against dawn.

Labrador Tea

Labrador leaves in a jar with a kerchief lid
release an arctic aroma when simmered on a stove.

Yesterday when fire broke out in the bosque,
the air had the stench of cauliflower in a steamer

when water evaporates and the pot scalds.
Although Apache plume, along with clusters of

western peppergrass, makes fragrant the wash,
owls that frequent the hole high up the arroyo's

bank have already come and gone. Yesterday,
though honey locust leaves shimmered

in a gust, no wasp nest had yet formed
under the porch. Repotting a *Spathiphyllum,*

then uncoiling a hose, I suddenly hear surf
through open slats of a door. Sprinklers come on

in the dark; a yellow slug crawls on a rain-
slicked banana leaf; as the mind flits, imbibes,

leaves clothed underneath with rusty hairs
suffuse a boreal light glistening on tidal pools.

Crisscross

Meandering across a field with wild asparagus,
I write with my body the characters for *grass,*
water, transformation, ache to be one with spring.
Biting into watermelon, spitting black seeds
onto a plate, I watch the eyes of an Armenian
accordion player, and before dropping a few
euros into his brown cap, smell sweat and fear.
I stay wary of the red horse, Relámpago, latch
the gate behind me; a thorned Russian olive
branch arcs across the path below my forehead,
and, approaching the Pojoaque River, I recall
the sign, Beware Pickpockets, find backhoe tracks,
water diverted into a ditch. Crisscrossing
the stream, I catch a lightning flash, the white-
capped Truchas peaks, behind, to the east, and in
the interval between lightning and thunder,
as snow accumulates on black branches,
the chasm between what I envision and what I do.

The Gift

The pieces of this jigsaw puzzle
will form King Tut's gold face,

but, at the moment, they are bits
of color strewn on the floor;

these moments of consciousness
have no jigsaw fit—heartbeat

of a swallow in flight, bobcat
prints across the Winsor Trail,

premonition that joy lurks inside
a match, uprooting sunflower stalks,

tipping an urn from a bridge
so that ashes form a cloud.

The pieces of a life stay pieces
at the end; no one restores papyrus

once it has erupted into flame;
but before agapanthus blooms,

before the body scorches, razes
consciousness, you have time

to puzzle, sway, lurch, binge,
skip, doodle, whine, incandesce.

Looking Back on the Muckleshoot Reservation
from Galisteo Street, Santa Fe

The bow of a Muckleshoot canoe, blessed
with eagle feather and sprig of yellow cedar,
is launched into a bay. A girl watches
her mother fry venison slabs in a skillet—
drops of blood sizzle, evaporate. Because
a neighbor feeds them, they eat wordlessly;
the silence breaks when she occasionally
gags, reaches into her throat, pulls out hair.
Gone is the father, riled, arguing with his boss,
who drove to the shooting range after work;
gone the accountant who embezzled funds,
displayed a pickup, and proclaimed a winning
flush at the casino. You donate chicken soup
and clothes but never learn if they arrive
at the south end of the city. Your small
acts are sandpiper tracks in wet sand.
Newspapers, plastic containers, beer bottles
fill the bins along this sloping one-way street.

Pig's Heaven Inn

Red chiles in a tilted basket catch sunlight—
we walk past a pile of burning mulberry leaves
into Xidi Village, enter a courtyard, notice
an inkstone, engraved with calligraphy, filled
with water and cassia petals, smell Ming
dynasty redwood panels. As a musician lifts
a small *xun* to his mouth and blows, I see kiwis
hanging from branches above a moon doorway:
a grandmother, once the youngest concubine,
propped in a chair with bandages around
her knees, complains of incessant pain;
someone spits in the street. As a second
musician plucks strings on a zither, pomelos
blacken on branches; a woman peels chestnuts;
two men in a flat-bottomed boat gather
duckweed out of a river. The notes splash,
silvery, onto cobblestone, and my fingers
suddenly ache: during the Cultural Revolution,
my aunt's husband leapt out of a third-story
window; at dawn I mistook the cries of
birds for rain. When the musicians pause,
Yellow Mountain pines sway near Bright
Summit Peak; a pig scuffles behind an enclosure;
someone blows his nose. Traces of the past
are wisps of mulberry smoke rising above
roof tiles; and before we, too, vanish, we hike
to where three trails converge: hundreds
of people are stopped ahead of us, hundreds
come up behind: we form a rivulet of people
funneling down through a chasm in the granite.

Retrieval

A train passes through the Sonoran Desert
when a sudden sandstorm at night sweeps
through the windows: everyone gags
and curses—sand, eddying under the dim
ceiling lights, lodges on eyelashes, clothes,
hair. Memory is encounter: each incident,

a bee thrumming in a hive. You catch
the aroma of incense in a courtyard
but fret you have sleepwalked for hours.
Observing grasshopper legs in a nook,
you brood then exult that a bat roosts
under the eave, yet fail to notice

quince fattening on branches, ache
that your insights may be white smoke
to flame. Though you note toothpicks
at a cash register, an elk head with antlers
mounted to the back of a passing trailer,
you are given a penlight but, within

minutes, misplace it. Without premonition,
striding up a cobblestone street,
through a Pátzcuaro doorway, you spot
a raised coffin with dissolving tapers
by each corner, and harbor a sting
then tang, wax then honey on the tongue.

Tesserae

Picking plums on a ladder, I notice a few
beyond my reach; our neighbor has replaced

the trampoline with cast-iron table and chairs;
black ants on the walkway are encircled

by a horde of smaller ones; we returned
to rose petals strewn on the bed; newly planted

cottonwoods curl at the leaf tips; once I
poked a pin through paper, raised and lowered

the sheet until a partial eclipse came into view;
as a child, I brooded over a *Life* photograph

of bodies piled up in Nanjing; koi mouth
the surface near a waterfall; hours earlier

we lay naked on a redwood deck; black ants
writhe, stiffen; along a south-facing slope,

I find red-capped *Russulas,* aspen boletes,
hedgehogs, a single death cap—deaths form

gaps, no, fissures, in my brain; you crack
a fortune cookie, "Water runs to what is wet."

In the Rose Light

no red-tailed hawk, no crows,
no geese, no raccoon tracks
by the door; when a magpie
flaps across the road,
disappears beyond the window
frame, I ponder frames—
glasses, doorjamb, beehive,
a moment of stillness—trace
an intimate geography:
son in Albany donating a cell
phone so that someone he
will never meet may call
911; clusters of wild irises
in the field; daughter glimpsed
through the doorway, arms
raised, in a ballerina pose,
then, in five minutes, asleep;
though the pink and orange
bougainvilleas are not yet
budding, I incandesce to
our firelight, to the ten years
we have entwined each other.

Qualia

"Oviparous," she says, "a duck-billed platypus
is oviparous." Strapped in her car seat,
she colors an array of tulips on white paper.
Stopped at a light on highway 285, he stares
at a gas station, convenience store. A man
steps out with a six-pack under his right arm,
while she repeats last night's queries:
Why does the Nile flow north? Who was Nefertiti?

And as cars accelerate, he knows the silver
one in the rearview mirror will pass him
on the right before he reaches the hilltop.
She sounds out "red": what was the shape
and color of a triceratops egg? Though
a chart can depict how height and weight
unfold along time, no chart can depict
how imagination unfolds, endlessly branching.

As sunlight slants over the Sangre de Cristos,
he notices Tesuque Pueblo police have pulled
a pickup off the highway. At school, lined
up for kindergarten, she waves, and he waves
back. As classmates enter, she waves; and again
he waves back, waves at apple blossoms
unfolding white along a studio wall, at
what is shed and slithering into pellucid air.

The Ginkgo Light

1

A downy woodpecker drills into a utility pole.
While you cut stems, arrange tulips in a vase,
I catch a down-bow on the A string, beginning
of "Song of the Wind." We savor black beans
with cilantro and rice, pinot noir; as light slants
through the kitchen window, spring is candlelight
at our fingertips. Ice crunches in river
breakup: someone shovels snow in a driveway,
collapses, and, hospitalized, catches staph
infection; out of airplane wreckage, a woman
identifies the ring on the charred corpse
of her spouse; a travel writer whose wife is in
hospice gazes at a lunar eclipse, the orange moon
at one-millionth of its normal brightness.
A 1300-year-old lotus seed germinates; a ginkgo
issues fan-shaped leaves; each hour teems.

2

A seven-year-old clips magenta lilacs for her mother;

"electrocuted tagging a substation";

patter of rain on skylight;

manta rays feed along a lit underwater cove;

seducing a patient,
he did not anticipate plummeting into an abyss;

over Siberia, a meteor explodes;

"I am happiest here, now!"

lesser goldfinch with nesting fiber in its beak;

love has no near or far.

3

Near Bikini Island, the atom bomb mushroomed
into a fireball that obsidianed the azure sky,

splayed palm leaves, iridescent black, in wind;
that fireball moment always lurks behind

the retired pilot's eyes, even when he jokes,
pours vodka, displays his goggles, medal,

leather jacket hanging from a peg. A woman
hums as she works with willow, X-Acto knife,

magnifying lens to restore a Jicarilla Apache
basket; she has no glimmer a zigzag line

is beginning to unravel, does not know within
a decade she will unload a slug into her mouth.

4

Through a moon gate, budding lotuses in a pond;

"You're it!"

he stressed rational inquiry
then drove south into the woods, put a gun to his head;

vaporized into shadows;

quince and peach trees leafing below the ditch;

succession and simultaneity;

the branchlike shapes in their sheets;

pizzicatti:
up the riv-er we will go.

5

August 6, 1945: a temple in Hiroshima 1130 meters
from the hypocenter disintegrates, while its ginkgo

buds after the blast. When the temple is rebuilt,
they make exit, entrance steps to the left and right

around it. Sometimes one fingers annihilation
before breaking into bliss. A mother with Alzheimer's

knows her son but not where she lives or when
he visits. During the Cultural Revolution,

Xu-mo scrubbed one million dishes on a tanker
and counted them in a trance. A dew point

is when a musher jogs alongside her sled dogs,
sparing them her weight on the ice to the finish.

6

Loaves of bread on a rack; a car splashes
a newspaper vendor on a traffic island.
On the road of days, we spot zodiacal light
above the horizon. Astronauts have strewn
footprints and streptococcus on the moon.
Chance sparks the prepared mind: a Cooper's
hawk perched on a cottonwood branch
quickens our synapses. In the orchard,
the sound of apricot blossoms unfolding;
mosquito larvae twitch water at the v-shaped
berm that pools runoff to the pond. We do
not believe we trudge around a flaming
incense burner on a road of years. As fireflies
brighten, we long to shimmer the darkness
with streamers. A pickup veers toward
then away, skewing light across our faces.

7

As light skews across our faces, we are
momentarily blinded, and, directionless,

have every which way to go. Lobelia
flowers in a patio pot; a neighbor

hands us three Bibb lettuces over a fence.
A cricket stridulates outside the window;

and while we listen to our exhale, inhale,
ephemera become more enduring than concrete.

Ginkgoes flare out. A jagged crack
spreads across windshield glass: we find

to recoil from darkness is to feed the darkness,
to suffer in time is—dichotomous venation—

to effloresce the time. One brisk morning,
we snap to layers of overlapping

fanned leaves scattered on the sidewalk,
finger a scar on wrist, scar on abdomen.

II

Spectral Line

1

Who passes through the gates of the four directions?
Robin coughs as she tightens a girth, adjusts saddle,
and, leading Paparazzo past three stalls, becomes
woman-leading-horse-into-daylight. Though the Chu
army conquered, how long does a victory last?
The mind sets sliver to sliver to comprehend, spark;
the mind tessellates to bring into being a new shape.
When the Blackfoot architect unveiled his master plan
with a spirit way leading to a center that opened
to the four directions, I saw the approach to
the Ming tombs, with pairs of seated then standing
lions, camels, elephants, horses lining the way.
I snapped when, through the camera lens,
I spotted blue sneakers—but not the woman—protruding
from the sides of a seated horse, and snapped
a white-haired woman with bound feet munching fry bread.
Peripheral details brighten like mating fireflies.
Then Gloria pointed to the east, gasped,
"Navajos will never set foot here: you've placed
these buildings in the ceremonial form of a rattlesnake."

Blinking red light on the machine: he presses
the button, and a voice staggers, "I'm back,"

"I don't know where I am," "I drive but can't
recollect how I get to where I am,"—whiteout

when a narwhal sprays out its blowhole and water
crystallizes in air—"thirty-three days."

He presses replay: the voice spirals, "I lost
four members of my family in a whaling accident";

he writes down numbers, 424-0590, dials,
"My cousin killed himself after his girlfriend

killed herself" ricochets in his ears; though
the name is blurred, he guesses at bowhead

ribs in a backyard, canisters of radioactive
waste stored inland on Saint Lawrence Island;

twenty below: Yupik children play string games;
when he broke the seal on a jar of smoked

king salmon, he recalled his skin and clothes
reeked of smoke from the float-house woodstove.

3

The stillness of heart-shaped leaves breaks
when a grasshopper leaps. I have never
watched so many inch along branches before.
Though they have devastated butterfly bushes,
they have left these lilacs unscathed, but can I
shrug, be marathoner-running-into-spring-light-
over-piñon-dotted-hills? The mind may snag,
still, weigh, sift, incubate, unbalance,
spark, rebalance, mend, release; when one
neighbor cuts grasses infested with grasshoppers,
inadvertently drives them into another's
organic farm loaded with beets, lettuce, basil,
carrots, kale, chard: we cannot act as if
we were asleep; do not entrench boundaries
but work to dissolve them. From light to dark
is a pass of how many miles? Together they sowed
dark millet and reclaimed the reed marsh.
As we entwine in darkness-beginning-to-trace-
light, dew evaporates off tips of grasses.

4

North they headed to Water Bend, what joy awaited them?

"I had to shoot myself or shoot someone else";

cries of snow geese in the wave of sunrise;

the secretary winked, "I'm wearing edible panties";

concubines were immolated on the emperor's death;

the green tips of a leafing apple;

"Here are instructions for when I am dead";

he was retracing the Long Walk;

when we addressed them as *tongzhi,* comrades, they laughed;

she swallowed the white sleeping pills and nearly OD'd;

the spring wind blew the ax off the chopping block;

when confronted with plagiarized lines, he shrugged, "I dreamed them";

the ex-marine checked staff desks at 8:20 for attendance;

from the south, elephants; from the west, horses; from the north, camels;

stepping through the miniature garden, they had no idea
they were writing the character *heart;*

she danced in a topless bar;

when the army recruiting film previewed in the undergound bomb shelter,
the crowd jeered;

she surprised him with a jar of Labrador leaves;

"Try to add to the sum total of human culture";

though the edges and angles are many, who knows their number?

5

Acoma Pueblo,

Diné,

Crow,

Oglala Lakota,

Menominee,

Northern Ute,

Zuni Pueblo,

Kiowa,

Muckleshoot,

Standing Rock Lakota,

Muscogee,

Ojibwe,

San Ildefonso Pueblo,

Comanche,

Tlingit,

Mescalero Apache,

Siberian Yupik,

Jemez Pueblo,

Pawnee,

Chugach/Alutiiq,

Mohawk,

Swampy Cree,

Osage,

Taos Pueblo,

Arapaho,

Jicarilla Apache,

Paiute,

Haida,

Onondaga,
Cochiti Pueblo,
Sioux,
Eastern Shawnee,
Caddo,
Santa Clara Pueblo,
Northern Cheyenne,
Prairie Band Potawatomi,
Choctaw,
Chickasaw,
Tsalagi,
Inupiat.

We forage for black and yellow morels
under tulip poplars, but they are camouflaged
on the forest floor. Wherever I squint,
I mark varicolored leaves, clusters of deer scat;
at first I zigzag a branch back and forth
under leaves, expecting to uncover some,
then learn to spot-check near the trunks,
forage farther out above the roots among
lichened rocks. We bring two dozen back,
sauté them, add to pasta, salad, sip wine;
but what coalesces in the body for weeks
are glimpses of blossoming redbuds while
driving along a road; horses by the second gate;
lights on the porch; a basket of apples,
bread, farm milk set at a downstairs table;
rocking horse upstairs; two tapers lit;
quicksilver kisses, a diamond light; and,
before, tremor when you felt something odd:
pulled a black tick off from behind your ear,
brushed a smaller one out of your hair.

7

Who rescues hunters tipped into arctic waters?
The hour is a cashmere scarf; as a black man

near a fountain raises saxophone to his lips
and showers the street with shimmering gold,

red lights of an ambulance weaving in traffic
bob into distance. From a dome, a pendulum

swings, almost touches numbers that mark
the hours in a circle on the floor. When

Robin's coworkers were terminated, she left
her telecommunications job to groom the horses

she loves, even in zero-degree weather; she
cinches a saddle on Nemo even now. A meadow

mushroom, covered overnight under a glass bowl,
releases, onto white paper, a galaxy of

chocolate brown spores. When you are still,
you spot the chance tracks of the living.

Who can suspend time on a string, make it
arc back and forth while earth rotates around it?

Incoming freshmen have been taken hostage,
the letter to the president began; we demand
computers and art supplies; limo service
to the Gathering of Nations; the sum total
of Pell funds released at once. Benildus Hall
is our headquarters. When the SWAT team
surrounded the building, someone pointed
to the small print: Happy April First.
The mind seizes a spore then releases it.
Descending into the Ming tomb, I discerned
electric lights; a cold iron railing;
people shuffling down steps; camera flashes;
people shuffling across, up the other side,
then out; but nothing was at the center;
only now—the moment when water from six
directions is water from the six directions.
A neighbor listens for wings before dawn;
plums begin to begin to drop from branches.

9

"A driver's door opened, and a head rolled
out of the burning car"—once she told me,

I could not expunge it. A backhoe beeps
when the driver moves it into reverse, beeps

above the din of morning traffic. A ginkgo
flames into yellow-gold, while, elsewhere,

red tulips flare on a slope. The mind weighs,
balances antinomies: at graduation, a student

speaker carries a black bag to the podium,
unveils bow, arrows, his entire body shaking,

and threatens to take aim at board members—
dissolves into air; a student in the audience

who slurs "far out" after every sentence
dissolves into air; the man who wafts eagle

feather above head, shoulders, along arms,
onto palms—dissolves into air; singers and

drummers who start and end dissolve into air;
and stillness, as we stir to dawn light, breaks.

The Double Helix

Marine biologists tracking pods of killer

whales in and out of Prince William Sound
recognize them by their dorsal fins and

by a flood of salmon scales swirling up.
A moose and two calves browse in twilight;

cow parsnip reeks along the road to Fritz Creek.

What does not dissolve in hindsight? The mind
tilts from starboard to port, port to starboard,

but steadies on even keel. Workmen stretch
an orange string to align flagstone steps,

stretch two lime green strings to delineate

the wall's thickness. Surveying stones
scattered on grass along the ditch, I observe

the wall rise in an irregular wave; and as
we dine at an oval table, discuss how

a diabetic homeopath endures unremitting pain,

how clusters of oyster mushrooms I forage
appear fresh but, when sliced, expose worms,

we lift and turn the incidents until—
a line of dorsal fins breaks water, blows

hang in air—we find their true and living place.

What neither comes nor goes? I try to converse
with a playwright who once sat in Oppenheimer's

chair; propped near a table, nodding before
a color TV—within reach of his right hand,

an oblong box of pills: A.M., noon, P.M., night—

while a slurry of news pours in, he struggles,
fails to string a single sentence, yet, when

I stand, gazes point-blank, extends an arm.
A line of yellow-groove bamboo extends

along a backyard fence. Yesterday we drove

into the Jemez Mountains, cut shaggymanes
along forest road 144, foraged among spruce

in mist and wavering rain, and though you
found a site where someone had cut

a bolete stipe and cap, though you spotted,

on a rock, as we drove past, a squirrel gnawing
a chunk of cèpe, we found nothing, but

reveled in the Douglas fir. Look out, look in;
what percolates in the dark? Clouds, rain;

we stretch and align ourselves, become one.

Cries of glaucous-winged gulls on the bay:
in the swirling light at summer solstice,

I mark a plethora in the twenty-five-foot
shift between low- and high-tide lines;

a man casts from shore, reels in small halibut;

red-faced cormorants nest in a cliff side;
an otter lazes with head above waves;

at low tide I wander among squirting clams,
make crunching noises stepping on shells,

flip a rock, find nudibranch eggs,

a gunnel fish; spot orange sea stars,
leather star, sculpin, frilled anemones,

a single moon jelly propelling through
water, worn crab shells at the entrance

to an octopus den, mating helmet crabs

below the tide line; but, before I know it,
the tide swerves back, starts to cover

the far shelf of exposed blue mussels;
gulls lift off; green sea urchins disappear

beneath lapping waves—my glimpse expires.

Skunks pass by a screen door in the dark;
once they ravaged ripening corn in our garden

and still crisscross us because a retired
violinist used to feed them. Once a composer—

a killer whale spyhops near a research vessel—

told a patron, "It's fine if you sleep with
my girlfriend," though he did not yet know

his out-of-town girlfriend had already dumped
him for a software engineer. We pick winesap,

braeburn, golden delicious apples in a neighbor's

orchard, press them; and as cider collects
in plastic jugs while a few yellow jackets sip,

time oozes. In a second I scramble
an egg, blink, scissor string, smudge

a photograph with blue ink, and the trigram

for water transforms into fire: when a former
soldier testifies that seeds contaminated

with plague were dumped from airplanes
during the growing season, a knife-edge runs

across my palms, but the truth scalds, anneals.

Fishermen fire at killer whales to prevent
them from stripping long lines of black cod.

You do not need to analyze toxins in peregrine
falcons to ascertain if the web is stretched

and stretched. In a Chimayo orchard where

two horses lean over a gate, two children
offer apples, while someone in a stream casts,

and the line snakes, glistens. Laughter
echoes from a table where someone pours

tequila onto ice, and ice crackles in a cup;

women slice sections of apples and toss them
in a wheelbarrow. We do not heed them

as we turn to each other and effervesce:
are we here to unravel, combust,

lightning the patch of ground where we stand?

Although the passions that torrent through
our bodies will one day vanish like smoke —

these words spiral the helix of living into smoke —
we embrace, rivet, inflame to mortal beauty,

to yellow-gold bursting through cottonwoods,

to morels sprouting through charred ground.
And as sky darkens, absorbs magpie nest,

green water tank, *canales*, pear, quince, slatted
wood fence, we tilt back and forth: though

the time we breathe is millennia when clocked

by a vibrating ray of cesium atoms, seconds
when measured by Comet Hyakutake — the tide

rushes over orange-tipped nudibranchs; silt
plunges underwater into a submarine canyon —

we observe snow on a flagstone path dissolve.

Equator

A bougainvillea thorn catches my sleeve
when I draw the curtain, then something
catches in myself. In Peru, Indians climb
a peak in late June to scan the Pleiades,
forecast the coming season. Meteorologists
have discovered El Niño causes high-level
November winds to blow from west to east,
and the Pleiades, visible low in the north-
east sky only as dawn appears, will dim.
I weigh blue nails, step up to a counter,
buy plastic cement, putty knife, gloves,
wrench, paint thinner—glance at my thumb
already stained black—have no way to
forecast year or hour. Lily pollen smeared
my shirt across the right shoulder when
I moved flowers out of the bedroom
for the night. I try to constellate points
by which I could, in clear weather, hike
across an immense lava flow, but find
elegy and ode our magnetic north and south.

Pinwheel

Firecrackers pop in bursts of white light and smoke;
a cymbal crash reverberates in air: mortality's

the incubator of dreams. Steaming green beans,
or screwing a wrought-iron hook into a post,

I do not expunge the past but ignite the fuse
to a whistling pinwheel. A girl sways under

a lion's head, while others undulate behind
in an *s*. Casting back eight years, we entwine:

a tulip sunlight flares along our shoulders.
At Pergamon, we cross a forecourt—in the center

stands a column bearing an Aesculapian snake,
the space we meander through called the incubator

of dreams. We did not foresee sponges dangling
inside a spice shop or the repeating pattern

of swastikas along walls that have led here.
Though it is Year of the Rooster, I pin *there*

to *here:* a line of dumplings, noodles, rice cakes
disappears; reverberating hail on the roof suddenly stops.

Power Line

As light runs along the length of power lines,
you glimpse, in the garden, watermelon,
honeydew, broccoli, asparagus, silking corn;

you register the tremor of five screech owls
perched on a railing under the wisteria,
shaggymanes pushing up through pecan shells;

though a microbiologist with a brain tumor
can't speak—he once intimated he most
feared to be waiting to die and is now

waiting to die—children play tag in spaces
around racks of bowling balls and white tables,
while someone scores a strike, shrieks;

young girls chassé diagonally across a floor;
a woman lays in an imperfection before
she completes her Teec Nos Pos weaving;

a sous-chef slices ginger, scallions,
anticipates placing a wet towel over dumplings,
as light lifts off the length of a power line.

Grand Bay

Gray Spanish moss hangs from the cypresses—
you stroll on an elevated boardwalk over dry swamp,

step off the platform and take a short path
to a green pitcher plant among grasses: it shows

signs of drought but is larger than your arms
can circle. The streaked pitchers resemble yearning

mouths opening at all angles, in all directions.
An alligator has flattened nearby horsetails,

but, famished, must have headed south.
When you take the boardwalk deeper in, climb

the latticed tower and gaze below, an airplane
lifts from a nearby strip and triggers vultures.

They rise in waves, while a lone hawk remains
unperturbed on a black gum branch. Over a hundred

vultures waver in the sky; while a few soar, most
circle, then resettle on branches. You meander

back out, graze the dangling Spanish moss,
find you choose not to avoid anything that comes.

Departures and Arrivals

An accountant leaning over a laptop
frets: *I have botched this, bungled that—*
he is not focused on numbers or accounts;
a taxi driver at an airport has no time
to contemplate rippling shadows of ginkgo leaves
but swerves between a van and truck;
a reinsurance analyst obsesses over a
one-in-ten probability that a hurricane

will scour the Florida Gulf Coast, while
an air-pollution expert is assigned
the task of designing an early warning
system for a dirty bomb. On an airplane,
waiting out a thunderstorm for two hours,
we cough, sneeze, shuffle, snooze,
flip through magazines, yet find
amethyst in an occasional vein of silence,

think *insulin*, sandpiper tracks on a beach;
and, when we least expect it, a peahen
strays into a yard; over a fence,
a neighbor passes a bag of organic lettuce
left over from farmers' market. As we doodle,
snack, brush spruce needles off caps
of boletes then place them in a grocery bag,
give them to friends, we gaze at a board

of departures and arrivals: Anchorage 2:45,
Boston 1:15, Chicago 11:50, Miami 3:10.
Each moment in time is a hub. In the airport

of dreams, why not munch waffles at midnight,
extemporize, ache, joke, converse with
the dead? *I'm out of it* snaps at the end
of a fiber-optic line, then *sizzles* at
how we thirst and renew our thirst in each other.

Fractal

Stopped at an intersection,
ruminating on how, in
a game of go, to consider all
the possible moves until
the end would take a computer
longer than the expected
lifetime of the universe,
you flit from *piccolo*
to *stovepipe* in a letter,
to scrutinizing faces
while standing in line
at the post office, to weather
forecast—a snowflake
has an infinite number
of possible shapes—
consider, only last weekend,
a wasp threaded along a
screen door in south light,
mark the impulse to—not
see this, do that—water
leafing pear trees along
a curved driveway, relax
the intricate openwork mesh
of spring, recall lifting
a packet of flax seeds
off the counter, and, checking
for an expiration date,
note—red light, green light—
sow when danger of
frost is past, then go, go.

The North Window

Before sky lightens to reveal a coyote fence,
he revels in the unseen: a green eel snaps,

javelinas snort, a cougar sips at a stream.
He will not live as if a seine slowly tightens

around them. Though he will never be a beekeeper,
or lepidopterist, or stand at the North Pole,

he might fire raku ware, whisk them to Atitlán,
set yellow irises at the table, raft them

down the Yukon. He revels at the flavor of
thimbleberries in his mouth, how they rivet

at a kiss. In an instant, raku ware and
the Yukon are at his fingertips. As light

traces sky out the north window, he nods:
silver poplars rise and thin to the very twig.

Yardangs

She who can't sleep takes a sleeping pill,
then another, and another. A crab apple
in the yard blossoms along the curve

of spring. Along a stone wall, we yearn
for a line of Japanese irises that does not appear,
glimpse a body on a stretcher loaded

into an ambulance. In the winter of spring,
a neighbor frets over air-pollution vectors;
a teenage girl worries her horse slashes

its neck along barbed wire. Prevailing winds:
west-northwest. As a physicist posits
all languages have a single root, I weigh

arête, yardang, strike valley, ciénega,
Tsé Bit'a'í: Shiprock, the rock with wings.
But is there bedrock? Scent of your

breasts and hair. Who is of the Bitter Water Clan?
A red tulip in a glass droops within hours.
Tremor at how *z, x, y* puts form into danger.

Virga

A quarterback slants a short pass to a tight end,
and the screen fills with tacklers.
                              He presses a button—
two miles deep in the Atlantic, shrimp hover around
a vent, where the ocean temperature is thirty-six
degrees—
                    sips a *lingzhi* mushroom brew, dozes:
at a banquet with wineglasses raised, the host starts
to say, "Long live";
                              teenage girls dressed in red silk
cartwheel past; a line of children trumpet on makeshift
horns;
              instrumental in fund-raising the construction
of an elementary school, he has journeyed north
of Yan'an.
                    Hunting wild ginseng in the hills is rain
that evaporates before it touches the ground;
                                        he has not
seen Orion for a month, nor Sirius, nor read they have
found signs of water on Mars.
                              Breathing is a struggle:
"I must live along a brightening curve, otherwise
it's fathomless dark";
                         he considers how his wife and son
will navigate, whether a cousin fencing tomb relics
will reinvent himself;
                              at an underwater peak
in the Coral Sea, shrimp thought to be extinct
for fifty million years, on a large screen, congregate.

After Completion

Mayans charted Venus's motion across the sky,
poured chocolate into jars and interred them
with the dead. A woman dips three bowls into
hare's-fur glaze, places them in a kiln, anticipates
removing them, red-hot, to a shelf to cool.
When samba melodies have dissipated into air,
when lights wrapped around a willow have vanished,
what pattern of shifting lines leads to Duration?
He encloses a section of garden in wire mesh
so that raccoons cannot strip ears in the dark,
picks cucumbers, moves cantaloupes out of furrows—
the yellow corn tassels before the white.
In this warm room, he slides his tongue along
her nipples; she runs her hair across his face;
they dip in the opaque, iron glaze of the day,
fire each emotion so that it becomes itself;
and, as the locus of the visible shrinks,
waves of red-capped boletes rise beneath conifers.

2

A sunfish strikes the fly
as soon as
it hits the water;

      the time of your life
      is the line extending;

            when he blinks,
            a hairlike floater
            shifts in his left eye;

      when is joy
      kindling to greater joy?

this nylon filament
is transparent in water
yet blue in air;

      grasshoppers
      rest in the tall grass.

3

Perched on a bare branch, a great horned owl
moves a wing, brushes an ear in the drizzle;
he can't dispel how it reeks of hunger as he
slams a car door, clicks seat belt, turns
the ignition key. Then he recalls casting
off a stern: he knows a strike, and, reeling in
the green nylon line, the boat turns; and as
a striped bass rises to the surface, he forgets
he is breathing. Once, together, using fifty
irregular yarrow stalks, they generated
a hexagram whose figure was Pushing Upward.
What glimmers as it passes through the sieve
of memory? For a decade they have wandered
in the Barrancas and grazed Apache plume.
He weeds so rows of corn may rise in the garden;
he weeds so that when he kisses her eyelids,
when they caress, and she shivers and sighs,
they rivet in their bodies, circumscribe *here.*

4

A great blue heron
perched
on a cottonwood branch;

tying
a Trilene knot;

a red dragonfly
nibbles the dangling fly
before he casts;

when he blinks,
he recalls their eyelashes;

casting
and losing sight
of the line;

the sky moves
from black to deep blue.

5

Ravens snatch fledgling peregrine falcons
out of a cliff side, but when they try to raid
a great horned owls' nest, the owls swoop,

and ravens erupt into balls of black feathers.
At Chichén Itzá, you do not need to stare
at a rack of skulls before you enter the ball

court to know they scrimmaged for their lives;
when the black rubber ball rebounded off
a hip up through the ring tenoned in the wall,

spectators shrieked, threw off their robes
and fled. The vanquished were tied into balls,
rolled down stone stairs to their deaths.

On one stela, a player lifts a severed head
by the hair, while the decapitated body spurts
six blood snakes. You become a black mirror:

when a woman pulls a barbed cord through
her tongue, when a man mutilates himself
with stingray spines, what vision is earned?

Lifting a tea bowl with a hare's-fur glaze,
he admires the russet that emerges along the rim;
though tea bowls have been named Dusk,
Shameless Woman, Thatch Hut—this nameless one
was a gift. He considers the brevity of what
they hold: the pond, an empty bowl, brims,
shimmers with what is to come. Their minds brim
when they traverse the narrow length of field
to their reclaimed pond: they have removed
Russian olives, planted slender cinquefoil,
marsh buttercup, blue iris, marsh aster, water
parsnip, riparian primrose, yellow monkey flower,
big blue lobelia, Yerba Manza; and though it
will be three to five years before the full effect,
several clusters of irises pulled out of mud,
placed on an island, are already in bloom.
A bullfrog dives, a bass darts into deep water
as they approach, while, above, a kingfisher circles.

7

They catch glimpses of trout in the depths,
spot two yellow ones flickering at a distance.

He thought a dead teal had drifted to shore,
then discerned it was a decoy. Venus rising

does not signify this world's end. In the yard,
he collects red leaves from a golden rain tree.

Here is the zigzag path to bliss: six trout align
in the water between aquatic grasses, wasps

nuzzle into an apple; cottonwood leaves
drift on the surface; a polar bear leaps off ice.

He does not need to spot their looping footprints
to recognize they missed several chances before

finding countless chanterelles in a clearing.
If joy, joy; if regret, regret; if ecstasy, ecstasy.

When they die, they vanish into their words;
they vanish and pinpoint flowers unfolding;

they pinpoint flowers and erupt into light;
they erupt and quicken the living to the living.

Notes

p. 15   *xun:* (Chinese) a ceramic musical instrument with holes

p. 48   *canales:* (Spanish) waterspouts off of a roof

p. 57   yardangs: desert landforms that usually occur in groups; they are narrow, steep-sided ridges carved from bedrock, with the ridges running parallel to each other and in the direction of the prevailing wind

p. 57   *ciénega:* (Spanish) swamp or marsh

p. 57   Tsé Bit'a'í: (Navajo) the rock with wings; the Navajo name for Shiprock, located in northwestern New Mexico

p. 58   *lingzhi:* (Chinese) the mushroom of immortality

About the Author

Arthur Sze was born in New York City. He graduated Phi Beta Kappa from the University of California at Berkeley and is the author of nine books of poetry. Professor emeritus at the Institute of American Indian Arts, he has conducted residencies at Bard College, Brown University, Mary Baldwin College, Naropa University, the University of Utah, and Washington University. His poems have been translated into Albanian, Bosnian, Chinese, Dutch, Italian, Romanian, Spanish, and Turkish. A recipient of two NEA fellowships, a Guggenheim Fellowship, a Howard Foundation Fellowship, a Lannan Literary Award, an American Book Award, a Lila Wallace–Reader's Digest Writers' Award, as well as grants from the Witter Bynner Foundation, Sze was the first poet laureate of Santa Fe, where he lives with his wife, Carol Moldaw, and daughter, Sarah.

The Chinese character for poetry is made up of two parts: "word" and "temple." It also serves as pressmark for Copper Canyon Press.

Since 1972, Copper Canyon Press has fostered the work of emerging, established, and world-renowned poets for an expanding audience. The Press thrives with the generous patronage of readers, writers, booksellers, librarians, teachers, students, and funders—everyone who shares the belief that poetry is vital to language and living.

Major funding has been provided by:

Anonymous

Beroz Ferrell & The Point, LLC

Cynthia Hartwig and Tom Booster

Lannan Foundation

National Endowment for the Arts

Cynthia Lovelace Sears and Frank Buxton

Washington State Arts Commission

For information and catalogs:

COPPER CANYON PRESS
Post Office Box 271
Port Townsend, Washington 98368
360-385-4925
www.coppercanyonpress.org

This book is set in two contemporary Dutch type-faces. The text face is Scala, by Martin Majoor. The titles are set in Legato, designed by Evert Bloemsma. Book design and composition by Valerie Brewster, Scribe Typography.

CPSIA information can be obtained
at www.ICGtesting.com
Printed in the USA
JSHW010920191219
3094JS00002B/15